CARTAGENA

CULTURAL ITINERARIES

AYUNTAMIENTO DE CARTAGENA
Concejalía de Turismo
Concejalía de Cultura y Educación

Región de Murcia
Consejería de Cultura y Educación
Dirección General de Cultura

Costa Cálida

© Textos: Ayuntamiento de Cartagena.
      Miguel Martínez Andréu, Alfonso Grandal López
© Diseño y maquetación: Gerardo Beniger
© Fotografías: Juan Manuel Díaz Burgos
© Traducción: Keith Gregor

Edita:
Ayuntamiento de Cartagena. Concejalía de Turismo.
      Concejalía de Cultura y Educación.

Imprime: I.G. Jiménez Godoy, s.a.

ISBN: 84-87529-24-0
Depósito Legal: MU-1.032/94

CONTENTS

ARCHEOLOGICAL ITINERARY

INTRODUCTION In antiquity, Cartagena was one of the most important and prosperous cities in the Iberian Peninsula, a fact borne out not just by ancient textual records but by its archeology.

This growth was the result of a combination of several factors, political and economic on the one hand, strategic on the other. The city's continuous development from its foundation, however, took place in a space restricted by a topography which, while aiding the initial growth, would later prevent all further expansion.

Indeed, through archeology we see how, in the same space, from the first native Iberian settlements to the present age, an intricate 2,500-year time-span packed with testimonies, there is a whole succession of stratigraphic developments, which without doubt constitute some of the city's most valuable cultural inheritances. A constant chain of episodes, orderly and rational on the one hand, ad hoc and even chaotic on the other, which steadily changed the city's appearance.

Founded by the Carthaginian general Asdrubal in 227 B.C., the city of Qart-Hadast (New City) would soon be absorbed by Rome after its conquest by Scipio, an event which marked the start of a long process of ajustment which would culminate in its recognition as a colony (Nova Carthago) in the year 44 B.C.

It would be in the period between the late 3rd century B.C. and the start of the 2nd century A.D. that the city experienced its greatest splendour. The period saw the realisation of major works of urban engineering and the conclusion of grandiose projects of civil and religious architecture.

Its privileged location, at the tip of a small peninsula surrounded by hills which opened on to the Mediterranean and a small lagoon stretching northwards, guaranteed an easy defence without relinquishing the huge potential of its port, exceptionally protected by a bay which reached right up to the gates of the city. Its proximity to the north of Africa, the excellent communications with the Meseta, Andalusia or the coasts of the Levant, and above all the enormous mining potential of the nearby sierras, ensured an ever-increasing commercial influence which would convert the colony into one of the most important cities in Roman Hispania.

Cartagena's soil bears the remains of these more prosperous time, but also the remin-

ders of the crises and upheavals which preceded its promotion as capital of one of the largest provinces of the empire under Diocletian. The Byzantine presence and the subsequent remodelling of certain sectors of the city; the tiny quarters which in the Visigoth and Hispanic-Moslem periods grew up on the ruins of what once were important Roman buildings; the medieval fortress, built on the old acropolis - for centuries, they would preserve the secrets of a history which only in the last few decades have archeologists begun to unveil.

Gravestones

MUNICIPAL ARCHEOLOGICAL MUSEUM

The Cartagena Municipal Archeological Museum is the head-quarters for all archeological activity in the city and neigh-bouring towns. The collections, some of them originating as long ago as the 16th century, grew steadily, if somewhat erratically, until they were eventually housed in a building be-longing to the Real Sociedad de Amigos del País. This buil-ding would be the germ of the first museum, founded in 1943 in part of an old construction in the present-day Plaza de Juan XXIII.

This date sees the beginning of a major reorganisation of the museum's exhibits, which for the first time were displayed in an orderly fashion. Meanwhile, the first systematic archeolo-gical studies in Cartagena commenced, studies which, espe-cially from the sixties and seventies on, would yield the first examples of underground conservation in the foundations of new buildings. This pioneering experiment would soon beco-me the model for all such archeological techniques in Spain.

The present-day installations, first opened in 1982, house the late-Roman necropolis of San Antón, a major late-4th cen-tury settlement; around the necropolis on two separate floors are the important collections displayed in the museum today. In an annex is the research centre, from which the diverse ar-cheological activities in the city are controlled and organised.

The various sections on the first floor are ordered chronologi-cally, beginning with the Prehistorical, which includes the dif-ferent cultural periods which left their mark on the area, from the mid-Paleolithic to the late iron age. The remaining sections trace the development of Roman colonisation, easily the most intense period in the city's development, with illus-trative finds from the old part and its environs. Of particular note is the abundant collection of epigraphs, one of the ri-chest in the peninsula, with a wide range of gravestones and

General view of museum.
Roman necropolis.

other religious and memorial pieces, as well as a variety of ceramics grouped chronologically according to the workshops where the were produced. This overview of Roman culture is completed by sections devoted to architecture and sculpture, as well as to commerce and industry.

Meanwhile, the second floor houses the most relevant pieces from some of the settlements explored, notably the township and Iberian necropolis of Los Nietos.

Also to be found here are apigraphs, coats of arms and ceramics, bringing us right up to the modern era. An audiovisual section gives extra information about the museum and the archeology of Cartagena.

CALLE DE LA MORERÍA BAJA

This is another of the important roads of the Roman period. Discovered 1957 at the start of work to the sewage system in this street, the archeological excavations carried out there helped preserve a small section with the remains of a road which must have led, via the present Puertas de Murcia, to one of the city's former entrances. As in the previous case, skirting the road are the masements of a colonnade for pedestrian traffic.

Remains of Roman dwelling.

CALLE DEL DUQUE, Nº29

This is another important find excavated in 1971 on the site of a future branch of the Caja de Ahorros de Alicante y Murcia. The same bank financed the exacation and subsequent preservation of the underground remains, which can now be visited during office hours.

The work resulted in the discovery of a stretch of road running from north to south ("cardo") and, underneath, the gallery of drains leading off from each of the dwellings.

There are pavements on either side of the road and, beyond them, the walls of the houses entered through doorways which steill preserve signs of the door fixing. A few rooms on the west side have floors decorated with geometrical motifs of the kind known as "opus signinvm". The visible remains date back to the age of Augustus.

Remains of road and Roman dwelling.

TORRE CIEGA

This monument, popularly known as the Torre Ciega ("Blind Tower") owing to its lack of any form of opening, is a Roman funereal building which dates back to the first century B.C. Dedicated to the memory of a figure called Titus Didius, the tower-like structure was part of a necropolis chich ran next to the main road into Carthago Nova. Its shape and the building technique used are based on contemporary Italic models, and the finish was achieved by embedding small stone points into the wet mortar, giving the surface the netlike appearance (opus reticulatum) so typical of Roman building.

Except for a few scant foundation stones, the rest of the monuments which formed the necropolis have disappeared with time, leaving the Torre Ciega as the sole survivor of the continual and ultimately fruitless pillaging of the treasure-hunters. Restored in 1960, the tower now stand as one of the most representative instances of Cartagena's archeology.

General view of remains of road and public building.

PLAZA DE LOS TRES REYES

Excavated in 1968, this sector is the first example of underground archeological preservation carried out in Cartagena. The monumental complex comprises a perfectly paved Roman road which linked the port area with the forum, and a large thermal area stretching under the present-day calle Honda as far as the first slopes of the el Molinete hill.

On the south side, flanking the road, are the basements of a colonnaded area which skirted one of the city's chief arteries.

Detail of road.

EXCAVATIONS AT ROMAN THEATRE

The northern side of the hill of La Concepción was one of the most densely populated spots in antiquity. In the first century B.C., scattered over its terraced slopes were the dwellings of a Roman residential quarter which, in the early years of the present era, was largely demolished to allow room for a monumental theatre, whose existence was established only recently.

The construction of this huge public edifice was a major feat of urban engineering which affected a sizeable sector of the city. The same rock which formed the hill was used as the base for the majority of the tiers of gradins.

After a chance discovery in 1987, the excavation work centred on the area of the scaena and the pulpitum. Later, the work extended to the orchestra and one of the side entrances of the theatre (itinera), where a monumental inscription was discovered. Meanwhile, further excavations around the pulpit have revealed remains of a late-Roman marketplace built over the rich architectural elements which formed the front of the stage, including a pair of marble altar slabs whose inscriptions have helped to establish the date of the theatre's construction.

Latin theatres were public buildings devoted to stage representations. There included genres such as tragedy, comedy, drama and farce, but also the reading of poetry and speeches by contemporary orators. The main function was, in a word, the staging of spectacles.

The memorial inscriptions found help us fix the date of the building of the Carthago Nova theatre around the end of the first century B.C. The monument was dedicated to the adopted son of Augustus, Gaius Caesar, who no doubt had important links with the colony's citizens and probably helped finance the works.

According to the epigraphic evidence, one of the city's chief personages, L. Ivnivs Paetus, promoted the construction, at a time when the city's growth was at its most vibrant, and when the search for a patron close to the imperial family, for the citizens' own political self-promotion and for the greater good of the city, was common.

Detail of access to gradins.

PUNIC RAMPART   The rampart was discovered in 1989, just off the Plaza del Almirante Bastarreche in one of the courtyards of the Hogar Escuela de "La Milagrosa", on the southern slopes of the Monte de San José, or the Aletes, as the southern slopes of the Monte de San José, or the Aletes, as the hill was known in Roman times. Its construction dates back to the end of the 3rd century B.C., some time around 277 B.C., the year the Punic city was founded by General Asdrúbal and Cartagena (Qart Hadast, in Punic) became the capital of Hispanic lands under Carthaginian control.

The architectural technique used in its construction follows the Hellenistic systems of fortification deployed throughout the central Mediterranean, especially Sicily and southern Italy, and could be classified as the "casemate" kind. The rampart comprises a system of parallel walls, almost 6 mts apart and built of sandstone rock joined at regular intervals by other walls or ties, leaving a series of inner rooms betwe-en both curtains, some with access to each other and to the centre of the fortification. Up above, covering the inner ro-oms or casemates, were the sentry posts. What is less clear is whether the rampart was endowed with merlons (and if so, what kind) or turrets.

Ancient sources suggest the rampart stretched all the way round the Punic city, though this section is the only evidence that exists at present. In the former layout of the city this construction would be located next to the isthmus, the only means of access to the city.

BYZANTINE RAMPART Excavations carried out in 1983 in the calle de la Soledad re-vealed massive walls, amongst which materials from the By-zantine period were found which led archeologists to believe its could be part of the walled area which protected the city, as described on the Comentiolus tablet.

The impotance of the find and the archeological value of the remains discovered spurred measures for their preservation in a specially prepared basement, which can now be visited un-der the Municipal Exhibitions Room.

Recent research in this area has permitted a more accurate account of its ancient historical evolution. The recent disco-very of the Roman theatre, a stone's throw away from the remains, has been decisive in this respect.

The earliest evidence of occupation in calle de la Soledad, da-ting back to the first century B.C., shortly before the building of the theatre, is a dwelling (domus) with parts of the rooms and their mozaic paving still remaining. Of special note is the emblem surrounding the drain of the atrium (the central courtyard), made out of tesseras nd fragments of marble, and adorned with four stylised dolphins at its corners.

The laying of the foundations for the colonnade bounding the garden which gave access to the theatre affected a large number of the dwellings which existed there, amongst them the dwelling in calle de la Soledad, which was literally cut off by the later work. The result was a curious collage effect, still visible today.

In the middle of the 6th century A.D. the new impulse given to the city's development by the Byzantines brought further reforms to the sector of the (by now) old theatre, with much of the existing material being pressed into service. The large foundations of the colonnade, slightly modified in parts, must have been re-used as a kind of rampart protecting a citadel which had folded back on the ruins of the ancient monument.

View of rampart and part of dwelling.

Detail of mozaic on floor.

AMPHITHEATRE The new status attained by the city after its designation as a colony in Caesar's time, and its transformation as the capital of one of the largest judicial areas in Hispania, brought about a huge urban development involving the restructurin of whole sectors and the occupation of areas which, up to then, had been practically uninhabited. One of the most striking develpments was the building of the Amphitheatre, which entailed the demolition of numerous dwellings of the modest quarter in the south-eastern section of the city.

This monument, one of the oldest of its kind in Hispania, was built around the middle of the 1st century B.C. along similar lines as its Italic precursors. Elliptical in shape, its longest axis measures 120 m. and its shortest, 90 m. The foundations are set on a bse of radial counterforts, some of which were revealed after excavations on the sections which protrude from under the present bull-ring, built in 1854 over the ruins of the ancient Roman edifice, which had been systematically pillaged from the very earliest times.

The two main entrances were at either end of the longer axis, their buttresses forming the vaults which supported the tiers of gra-

dins. At more elevanted points of the base rock, a section of the gradins was cut directly into it, the rest of them being completed with mortar and stone work.

Inside the amphitheatre, under the centre of the ring, there was a ditch which would occasionally be filled with water to represent naval battles. The water flowed away through a (well preserved) system of channels linked to the main drains.

Apart from the naumachias, the most popular events would be fights between wild beasts and gladiator combats.

For the building of the amphitheatre a range of different materials was used. The most common of these was the sandstone from the town of Canteras and the andesite and other volcanic rock from the hills around Beaza and Ventura. All of these towns were close to Cartagena.

NACIONAL MUSEUM OF MARITIME ARCHEOLOGY

NATIONAL MUSEUM OF The National Museum of Maritime Archeology and National Centre for Underwater Archeological Research, both dependent on the Ministry of Culture, were founded jointly on the 9th June 1980. The aim of both was to coordinate activities aimed at preserving and investigating the historic and artistic heritage concerned with the sea. The Museum finally opened its doors to the public in 1982.

The rooms of the Museum, divided into four main areas, contain archeological material from the sea and wrecks, which supply important evidence for research into the routes of the former sea traffic.

Area I displays a large amount of the amphoras made in ancient times, from the Phoenicians to the Romans, for the transportation of a wide range of merchandise.

Of special relevance in Area II area the materials from several wrecks, especially the "Bajo de la Campana" (Isla Grosa), with its cargo of inscribed ivory, and the "San Ferreol" of the Roman Republic.

A large part of Area III is occupied by the exhibition of different pieces of naval architecture, including a full-sized reconstruction of a section of a Roman merchant ship.

Apart from certain exhibits of sea traffic, the last Area includes models and illustrations

tracing the development of shipping in the Mediterranean basin up to the High Middle Ages.

Roman merchant ship.

CASTLE OF LA CONCEPCIÓN

The castle of la Concepción is to be found on the hill of that name, known in antiquity (according to the writer Polibius) as Mount Esculapius.

The first reports of its existence date back to the Reconquest, though the materials with which it was built are known to have come largely from other constructions existing there when the city was still a Roman colony, and which had been renovated in the Hispanic-Moslem period.

It seems that in the times of Henry II (1390-1406) there was a major reconstruction in which massive ashlars from the old amphitheatre were also employed. From the 16th century on, there are more and more reports concerning the ill state of repair of the castle and the frailty of its defences, as well as the inefficacy of the continual reparations carried out at the time. All the same, it continued to be Cartagena's securest point and a privileged place from which to receive signals from the coastal watchtowers and to sound the alarm when danger was near.

In the second half of the 18th century, once the building of new castles and ramparts surrounding the city had removed its defensive function, it was abandoned and fell into ruin. Only a lack of funds saved it from demolition.

In the 19th century it would be the dispute over ownership of the lands between the State and the Ayuntamiento which deferred demolition. But the cession of the castle to the city in 1915, in the times of the mayor Alfonso Torres, opened the way for the final redevelopment of the area. The work begun in 1924, and finished in 1930, left as the sole recognisable remnant of the former building the half-demolished main buttress or "tower of homage", with its gothic window and winding stairs, as well as the tower which guarded the main access (Puerta de la Villa). The remainder was converted into a park, following the desing of the architect Víctor Beltrí.

Nonetheless, the castle was not forgotten by the people of Cartagena and began to be called the "castle of ducks", owing to the ducks which lived on the lake in the park. In the eighties, the area fell into dereliction as a result of the steady decline of the urban area surrounding it, though the years 1993 and 1994 hve seen a recovery due to major restoration work, including the first step towards a revaluation of the former structures of the castle which were hidden by the reforms carried out in the twenties.

Stairs up to tower.

View of inside
the old cathedral.

CATHEDRAL OF SANTA MARÍA LA VIEJA

The history of the old cathedral, as a place of Christian worship, begins in the late 13th century. From that time on, practically up to the present, the temple we know today has undergone such a great variety of changes that the inherent architectural value of its crumbling naves is complemented by that of its history.

Steeped in legend, every corner of the cathedral has evoked a different story with which popular belief, ever alive to the city's vast historic inheritance, has lit the darkest centuries of Christendom. It is no surprise, then, that the apostle St Jame should once have come here, nor that the two enormous Roman shafts which guard the apse should invoke the existence of both an unknown praetor and the matyrs who spilled their blood on the column to which they were tied.

Indeed, in the old cathedral, temple and history merge to form an indissoluble whole. A large number of the walls were raised with ashlard from the Roman theatre and other ancient building which surrounded it; one of the crypts, excavated under the cathedral, preserves the decorative paving of a 1st century B.C. "domus". Its very location and the extensions made to the temple would be at the expense of the gradins of the old Pagan edifice.

It is likely that this same spot was once occupied by the Moslem mosque, reconverted into a church in the 13th century when the city was conquered by the Crhistians. For a few years it would be the seat of the Cartagena bishopric, until the latter was shifted to Murcia to accompany the bishop, who had abandoned a city which was too poor and too prone to attack by land and sea (by Granadans, Valencians, Berebers, etc.).

All that remains of the medieval period are a few re-used ancient columns, part of the tower and the west wall where the original entrance stood. Of the original central nave only the most westerly edge of the Gothic vaulting has been preserved.

The chapel of the Cuatro Santos is 16th century, the work of the military engineer Juan Bautista Antonelli in 1571, when he came to the city to design its ramparts. The chapel of the Cristo Moreno was built in 1691 under the patronage of the Duke of Veragua, don Pedro Manuel Colón de Portugal de la Cueva y Enriquez, whose arms appear on the arch bove the entrance. The chapel is covered by an eight-sided dome over an octagonal drum, which is rare for the region. Both the arch and the dome are richly decorated with plaster motifs of plants and cherubs.

Santa María la Vieja was never well maintained and was largely abandoned for many years (in 1777 the parish switched to Santa María de Gracia). Finally, between 1899 and 1904, the church was rebuilt by the architect Víctor Beltrí in the "medieval" style, neo-Romanic on the outside and neo-Gothic on the inside. Eventually, the destruction brought by the Civil Was and final abndonment left the temple completely ruined.

Main entrance to temple.

BAROQUE AND NEOCLASSICAL ITINERARY

INTRODUCTION   In the 18th century Cartagena attained one of the high
points in its history. This moment of prominence was the result of different factors dating back to the 17th century,
though no doubt the deciding one was the choice of Cartagena in 1728 as the capital of the maritime department of
the Mediterranean. As a consequence of this choice, there
would be an extraordinary development of the already emer-
gent naval base, with the creation of a large arsenal (1744)
and a whole series of important complementary military
constructions (ramparts, castles, barracks, hospital, offices,
prison etc.).

Virtually all of these works were built during the fruitful
resign of Charles III (1759-1788) and owe much to the
initiative of the Count of Aranda, commander in chief for
Valencia and Murcia.

Parallel to the military and economic growth, there was a
dramatic rise in the city's population, from 10,000 to 50,000,
in the space of a hundred years. This rise brought about the
renovation of the existing public buildings and the construction of new ones, all of them enriched with numerous works
of art. Regrettably, very little of the civil and religious art of
the period has been preserved, at least in comparison to the
importance and interest of the military architecture.

The buildings selected for commentary below are all to be
found in the old part of the city; not included in this guide
are other interesting examples in the quarters, such as the
churches of San Antón and Santa Lucía, and in the hills surrounding the city, such as the cstles of Galeras, los Moros
and la Atalaya.

Dome over crossing.

Façade and entrance to church.

CHURCH OF EL CARMEN

This temple was the church of the former convent of San Joaquín, belonging to the barefooted Carmelites, which was made into the parish church in 1887.

The building has a two-bodied façade with fronton interrupted by the bell tower, with its striking mixture of classical and popular elements. The colonnade is a transitional space between the exterior (itself separated from the street by a flight of steps and gate) and the interior of the temple. The latter has a single nave with lateral chapels and crossing covered by a dome with an undulated cornice, a feature which is rare in the region's baroque inheritance. At the end of the nave is the choir loft and, below that, the narthex covered by vaulting over an arcade which has five opening on to the atrium, in the manner typical of Carmelite constructions in Madrid.

View of main nave to choir.

Main nave of church.

SANTA MARÍA DE GRACIA

Erected from 1712 on lands belonging to an old 16th century hermitage, the cathedral was developed all through the 18th century and underwent major reforms in the 19th and 20th centuries. The façade is still unfinished.

The originl design was for a cathedral-size church which, with three naves, crossing, lateral chapels and apse aisle, would be the natural successor to the church of Santa María la Vieja, in the hope of recovering for Cartagena the bishopric which had been lost in the 13th century and had been claimed by the city from at least the 16th on. By 1777 half the plans were completed and the parish shifted to the new church. However, for the building of the upper end the ambitious original design was forgotten and the chancel was built where the crossing was meant to be, while the planned main chapel and apse aisle disappeared altogether. These changes have left their mark on the final result, a rat-

Façade.

her outsized and ill-lit space, whose sheer proportions, however, show the scale of the original project.

The chapels, with their beautiful domes and some 18th cnetury frescos, are where the most valuable architectural elements are to be found. The most striking of them is the chapel of the Cristo de Medinaceli (before the Virgen del Mar), with an original dome over a drum with undulated cornice.

Amongst the sculptures to be found inside, the most outstanding are the medieval image of the Virgen del Rosel, the former patron of Cartagena, and the Four Saints carved by Salzillo. The same sculptor also produced the sleeping apostles in the Oración del Huerto and the wounded executioner in the Osculo, which can be admired in the Californian chapel of the Prendimiento, and which, together with many other fascinating sculptures, are displayed in the Easter processions which, since the 18th century, have set out from this church.

Chapel of christ of Medinaceli.

Windows.

Building seen from foot of Muralla del Mar.

ESCUELA DE GUARDIAS MARINAS

The building is presently the site of Navy Headquarters, but it was designed in 1785 by the great neoclassical architect Juan de Villanueva as a school and barracks for marines. The construction and possibly the final design were shared by other arcitects and engineers, notably Simón Ferrer y Burgos. Though the building has not undergone too many modifications since its construction, the reforms have partly disfigured the top floor, which is somewhat discordant with the rest. The modern constructions which have sprung up around it have also diminished the building's former preeminence over the original row of two-and three-floor houses.

Bulwark of rampart.

MURALLA DEL MAR

An essential part of the defences for the arsenal and plaza de Cartagena, this rampart was commissioned by Charles III and built under the direction of the military engineers Francisco Llobet and Mateo Vodopich. It had three main gates: the Muelle (between the plaza del Ayuntamiento and the plaza de los Héroes de Santiago de Cuba y Cavite), the San José (in the present-day plaza de Bastarreche) and the Madrid (opposite the plaza de España). The only part remaining is the stretch between the former Muelle and San José gates and, outside the city, the defences of the Arsenal.

It was built in solid rubblework, on foundation stones of a rock known as atabaire, and reinforced at corners and salients with ashlars of the far more erosion-resistant pinto variety.

In 1891, once it had lost all defensive value, the wall began to be dismantled, a process which sped up after 1990 (with the demolition of the Muelle gate) and concluded in 1902. 1915 saw the installation of gardens on the top of the muralla del Mar and the replacement of the original parapet with a balustrade.

CAPITANIA GENERAL

The building was constructed in 1740 to plans by the military engineer Pedro Feringán on part of the large land occupied by the Casa del Rey, seat of the Proveeduría de Armadas y Fronteras during the 16th and 17th centuries, which had long fallen into disuse.

The main façade waas rebuilt in the 19th century and remodelled in the 20th, with the suppression of the typical miradors which adorned it and an emphasis on more classicist elements. Official residence of the commander of the Mediterraneam Maritime Zone, the building receives important visitors and its interior is richly decorated. Of special note is the imperial staircase and the main floor.

El Parque - as it is known in Cartagena - was, by all accounts, designed by the military engineer Mateo Vodopich and consists of four bodies and two courtyards. It was practically destroyed in the explosion at the end of the canton uprising in 1874, and it was not properly rebuilt till the beginning of the present century. The main façade was greatly modified, since an upper floor was added and the original rubblework, which gave the building the appearance of a fortress (an effect enhanced by the thick grills covering the huge windows), was plastered over. Nonetheless, the southern and western façades, though highly delapidated, give a better idea of the building's original appearance.

Inside, the most outstanding aspects are the spherical and ribbed brick vaults on pillars and the Sevillian-tiled courtyard.

PARQUE MAESTRANZA DE ARTILLERÍA

PUERTA DEL ARSENAL

Of the gates to the walls of Cartagena built in the 18th century, this is the only one that remains standing. Conceived as the monumental entrance to the Arsenal - the most important of all the works carried out in the city in the 18th century -, in 1865 an elegant clock tower, the work of the engineer Tomás Tallarie, was added to it (yet nother indication of the importance of the space to which it gives access).

This large and solid edifice was planned by the military engineer Sebastián Feringán. The well-known health problems affecting Cartagena at the time made this one of the first works to be completed after the city's conversion into the main Spanish naval base on the Mediterranean.

It is composed of two bodies with their corresponding courtyards, covering large undergroun water cisterns, with ground floor, two upper floors and huge garret-like lofts. Initially it could hold 4,000 patients and as many as 9,000 during the outbreak of yellow fever in 1804. Nevertheless, the usual occupation was far lower, and a large number of its installations were used variously as dwellings, storehouses and a barracks.

The whole complex has been subject to numerous modifications and reforms to adapt to the different uses and to medical advances, though most of these reforms have taken place on the inside and have hardly affected the building's external appearance. The mid-19th century reforms were on a grand scale and, amongst other improvements, at the beginning of the 20th century (1913) a clearly modernist-style monumental marble staircase was built, some ceilings were decorated with allegorical paintings by Siles and the walls were skirted with Sevillian-style and modernist tiles. The last great reforms were made in the 1960s.

MILITARY HOSPITAL

In 1984 the hospital left its age-old site for a new location, as a result of which the former building fell into rapid decline. However, it is soon to be restored as it is to become a centre for the university studies on offer in Cartagena.

MODERNIST AND ECLECTIC ITINERARY

INTRODUCTION

Between 1874 (the end of the cantonal war) and the First World War Cartagena enjoyed a period of great economic prosperity, the fruit, above all, of the boom in mining which, in turn, stimulated the development of other industries and commerce. This widespread economic boom is reflected in the proliferation of new and costly buildings, both public and private, and in the projection of a carefully organised suburban development.

But if increased wealth was the requisite for such large-scale projects, their architectural success depended on the existence of brilliant ideas and the men capable of carrying them out. The ideas would come mainly from the modernist style which, above all via Barcelona and, to a lesser extent, Madrid, would soon reach Cartagena, where the novelty and optimism of the new style would soon take a strong hold. What is plain, however, is that, most of the time, moderninsm would be seen in a multitude of decorative elements which enriched the eclectic bases to which they were added, and had more of an impact in the interiors than on the façades.

There was also no shortage of fine architects capable of absorbing the new international currents, and first amongst them Víctor Beltrí (Tortosa, 1865-Cartagena, 1936), author or collaborator in most of the finest examples of modernism to be found in Cartagena.

The buildings presented briefly below are all situated in the old part of Cartagena or its immediate surroundings; they are the most characteristic of the many that were built in the last decades of the 19th century and first of the 20th, but are by no means the only interesting ones. It is enough to stroll through streets and squares such as the calle Mayor, las Puertas de Murcia, the calle del Carmen, Jabonerías, Jara, or the plazas San Francisco and la Merced, to appreciate a host of buildings which are a magnificent display of the quality attained by Cartagena's architecture in the years in question. Nor can one neglect further examples is the suburbs, quarters and countryside, many of them of great interest.

Main altar with carving of Virgen de la Caridad.

CHURCH OF LA CARIDAD

This temple was the church of the la Caridad hospital which, before moving to its present location in the los Barreros quarter, occupied the whole block. The present form was the design of the engineer Tomás Tallaríe in 1893, with its neo-classical style on a metal structure, which is a sign of the new era.

The building is centre-structured, with a dome over a drum which, highly visible from the highest points of the city, is unmistakeable with its half-Michael, Angeloesque, half-Central European appearance. The interior, dominated by the cupola, is reminiscent of many neoclassical buildings, themselves based on the Roman Pantheon of Agrippa. The façade is arch-shaped, with columns and Corinthian pilasters.

As a result of its monumental structure, the church of la Caridad soon became the city's main temple, the worthy home of its patron, the Virgen de los Dolores, whose image is known as the Virgen de la Caridad. The image is a highly beautiful early-18th century Neapolitan piety. From the same century there are several admirable sculptures by Salzillo and his school, such as the crucified Christ, St Francis and St Anthony of Padua, the group of the Virgen de los Remedios, St Joseph, St John of the Cross and San Ginés, the latter three on the remarkable rococo altarpiece in the communion chapel. As far as paintings are concerned, there is an outstanding Immaculate by Ara, a disciple of Murillo's, and a St Francis of Assisi from the Ribera school, both from the 17th century, as well as the impressive series of canvasses by Manuel Wssel de Guimbarda in 1893, some of them of huge proportions.

Christ crucufied.

Group of image of Virgen de los Remedios.

Detail of façade.

HOTEL DE LA COMPAÑÍA DEL ENSANCHE

Designed by the architect Tomás Rico as an office and dwelling, this was one of the first buildings to be built during the Development. Its striking modernist features, exemplified by the magnificent mirador overlooking the façade and the carved pinion which dominates it, were intended as a way of promoting the area in which the city was to enlarged. For the rest, despite the unequivocally modernist air given by the mirador, the building is mainly eclectic in composition and almost all of its decorative details.

Main façade.

CASA CLARES This building is the first and most important of the ones designed by the Cartagena architect Mario Spottorno. Of its two façades, the more decorative and relevant one looks onto the calle del Aire, where the modernist style is especially evident in the cornice and glass windows, as well as the floral details. Equally worthy of note are the bulbous capitals on the ground-floor pillars.

Main façade.

Main entrance to building.

RAILWAY STATION

The building was designed by the engineer Rafael Peryoncely. The academic eclecticism is typical of the style of engineers in the period, though there are modernist decorative elements such as the ironwork on doors and columns and, above all, the graceful canopy over the main entrance. The outstanding part of the façade is the central body, dominated by a large thermal window topped by a clock presiding over the whole.

The interior was also modernist in style, though today all that remains of the original are the ticket windows, the ironwork, the vaulted ceiling and the lamp. There was no metal structure over the platforms; instead, they were covered by a simple canopy which now no longer exists.

Detail of entrance.
Station interior.

Detail of façade.

CASA CERVANTES

With this, his first great work, the architect Víctor Beltrí laid the foundations of modernism in Cartagena. Situated in the most visible spot in the calle Mayor, the dimensions and character this building possesses allow it to stand out from the rest, including the casino which, situated next door, goes almost unnoticed, despite its striking appearance.

The façade - the only part which remains of the original construction - is crowned with a curved fronton over the main entrance and incorporates at either end of the main floor and second floor the white miradors so typical of Cartagena, and presents a classic axial composition. In a clear allusion to the origin of the fortune of the house's first owner, the mining empresario Serafín Cervantes, symbols relating to commerce, industry and mining, starting with the bronze plaques with the heads of Mercury and Minerva adorning the front door, abound on the façade.

General view of building.

CASA AGUIRRE

Situated at a spot which offers an extraordinary view, between the crowded plaza de la Merced and the long, straight and much frequented calle de San Diego, the building's architect, Víctor Beltrí, harnessed this visual potential and built on the very same corner a projecting tower, crowned with a shining dome and decorated with a first-floor mirador. Running off the tower there are two façades, the main one looking on to the square and the other on to the calle de San Diego. Both the façades and the tower are profusely decorated, especially at the top, with rococo-style ceramic motifs. Bees, the symbol of industry, stand out on the tower as a kind of blazon for the wealthy mining empresario who commissioned the dwelling. The interior, of which only the hall, living-room, staircase and study are preserved in their original form, was decorated in the same rococo-based modernist style, except for the chapel, which is neo-gothic.

**Detail of main
entrance.**

**General view
of palace.**

Gallary on main façade.

Stairs to first floor.

AYUNTAMIENTO Designed by Tomás Rico, the three façades of this triangular building are quite distinct. The main façade, which looks on to the plaza del Ayuntamiento, it set off by means of a colonnade and dome which mark the entrance and location of the sessions room, which opens out onto the massive balcony over the colonnade. On the corner of this façade, which looks on to the plaza de los Héroes de Santiago de Cuba y Cavite, stands the clock tower with its dome and belfry, where one can find the Mayor's Office, the most important part of the building together with the sessions room. The construction is eclectic and classicist, somewhat Frenchified, in style, and is intended to emphasise the official and representative nature of the edifice.

Inside, the outstanding elements are the hall and magnificent imperial staircase, where the modernist style, hinted at in certain details on the exterior, is plain to see. Of equal note are the paintings and decorative details in the area of state in the hall andon the first floor, as well as the paintings by Wssel de Guimbarda, Vicente Ros, Portela, etc., which adorn the walls.

Hall.
Mayor's office.

Detail of interior.
Access to first floor.

CASINO The eighteenth-century front reminds us of the origin of the building, the former house of the Marquis of Casatilly, remodelled on different occasions and definitively by Víctor Beltrí around 1897. For the façade the architect was inspired by the electic works of Vilaseca, especially as far as the upper section is concerned. The ground floor, presided over by the monumental portal, is occupied by large "fish bowl" salon windows. There are five balconies on the first floor, the one over the main entrance being the most ornate. On the top floor the windows alternate with allegorical medallions representing the arts, war, industry, commerce and the sciences.

Inside, the most striking feature is the windowed courtyard surrounded by a first-floor gallery. As far as the decoration of the different rooms is concerned, the dominant trait is modernism, as well as the furniture contained within them. All of the original elements are of great value, as is to be expected in this, the most representative edifice of the local bourgeoisie.

General view.

CASA MAESTRE

The rich and influential José Maestre contacted the Barcelona architect Marcelino Coquillat y Llofriu, from whom he commissioned a dwelling which would surpass the sumptuous mansions being constructed at the time in Cartagena by other well-to-do industrialists. Coquillat's design was overseen by the local architect Víctor Beltrí.

The façade of the building, the only part preserved as it was designed, was inspired by the Casa Calvet by Gaudí, which in turn is clearly reminiscent of the baroque. It differs, however, in its construction around a central axis, clearly visible from the remarkable door with its rococo decorations, the beautiful mirador and its windows, to the very top of the building. Equally original is the ternary rhythm in which these elements appear and which is repeated in the combination of the remaining openings, as well as the large, typically modernist, circular window.

This building would have an enormous influence on Cartagena architects and, in particular, Beltrí.

General view.

CASA DORDA The main façade of this house (it has another smaller on which gives on to the calle Jabonerías) was planned by Víctor Beltrí under the influence of the baroque, as shown by the curved finials adorned with mouldings and floral patterns. It is hard to say, however, to what extent this influence is a direct on or an adaptation of the Catalan modernist neo-baroque, represented in Cartagena by the Casa Maestre, from which certain elements, such as the main balcony, are clearly copied.

As far as the interior is concerned, the most interesting feature is the large Arabian-style central courtyard, with elements taken from the mosque in Córdoba and the Alhambra in Granada.

Detail of staircase.

General view of inner courtyard.

Main entrance
with gardens.

Inner
courtyard.

CASA ZAPATA The Zapata family owed its fortune, like almost every other Cartagena family in the period, to mining. The house designed for them by Víctor Beltrí was built on a privileged spot: in the plaza de España, between the Alameda and calle 18 del Ensanche, occupying a whole block. The house is a villa surrounded by a picturesque garden enclosed behind a beautiful wall. The building is in the gothic-inspired modernist style so frequent in Catalonia, where the architect was born. The gothic-style medievalism is especially noticeable in the windows and battlemented tower, which contrast with other elements such as the elegant zinc covering over the central tower, the colonnaded porch, the rear galleries or the beautiful Viennese-style finials on the outer wall. These elements give the building an eclectic and cosmopolitan touch which softens the dominant Catalan neogothic style.

Inside the building, there is a magnificent courtyard covered by glass plates; Arabaic in style, the decoration is reminiscent of the Alhambra in Granada on which it is based.

Nowadays, the Casa Zapata, easily one of the finest examples of modernism in Cartagena, has been converted into a school and is half-hidden behind later constructions which, moreover, have done away with most of the garden and a large section of the outer wall.

GRAN HOTEL This magnificent building was designed by Tomás Rico who was able to oversee the construction until his death in 1912; afterwards, Víctor Beltrí took over the direction. Of the original project, Beltrí kept the structure and several details in the construction of the first three floors, but finished it off in a highly personal and striking way, making the building, in the words of Pérez Rojas, the most cosmopolitan construction in the whole region of Murcia. The Gran Hotel is a reflection of the harmonious interpretation of Viennese and French modernist influences (highly visible on the final floor), at a time when the style was beginning to fall out of fashion, even in Cartagena. The hotel's location, at the corner of the narrow calles Jara and del Aire, opposite the plaza de San Sebastián, was cleverly exploited by Rico, who built onto the vertex where the two façades meet in an acute angle an elegant rotunda crowned with a striking dome. The rotunda strengthens the impression of the prow of a huge ship which one gets looking up from the square.

To break the monotony of six identical floors, there is a play on the colours white and red and a different treatment of each of the floors (only the third and fourth are the same), with continuous balconies alternating with individual ones and a multitude of elegantly designed decorative details, especially the ironwork on doors and canopies.

Detail of entrance.

Windows.

CASA DEL NIÑO

Víctor Beltrí, who was the architect of the Child Protection Society building, designed the Casa del Niño, which was begun in 1917 and later enlarged by Lorenzo Ros. The different bodies which were built eventually occupied the whole block, and so helped to develop what was then a marginal district of the city.

Beltrí's style attains here a simplicity and a harmonisation of a Viennese influence fully assimilated and redirected, all of which makes this building possibly his purest work. It is to the credit of Lorenzo Ros that he was able, twelve years later, to blend into the design the classrooms erected in the courtyard, taking his inspiration from the same tradition of Viennese modernism.

General view of courtyard.

Detail of ornamentation.

Main façade.

CASA LLAGOSTERA   The construction of this house was entrusted to Víctor Beltrí by the Catalan-born merchant Llagostera, who kept the first floor for his own private residence. The most interesting feature of the construction is, without doubt, its extraordinary façade, which has been described (Pérez Rojas) as the most beautiful and original in 20th century Murcian architecture. All superfluous elements were eliminated from it and it was reduced to the traditional Cartagena model based on central balconies and lateral miradors. The decoration consists entirely of the magnificent ceramics of Gaspar Polo; it could even be said the façade was designed as a simple pretext for the ceramic work. As well as flowers and garlands, the tiles show the allegorical figures of Minerva and Mercury (the god of commerce) and the shields of Barcelona and Murcia (on either side of Minerva), as well as those of Cartagena and Man-lleu (flanking the figure of Mercury).

At such a late stage as 1916, the modernist influence is by now quite weak, though it is still perceptible in the vegetable decorations and the "feeling" exuded by the building.

General view of palace.

This mansion was commissioned by the wealthy industrialist Andrés Pedreño and designed by the architect Carlos Mancha, and it is his most accomplished work. Exceptionally sited at the very Puertas de Murci and between what were, even more so than today, two main streets, Jabonerías and el Carmen, it has all the appearance of a Renaissance palace. Running across the main façade (the most interesting one) is a large first-floor balcony, adorned with kylins (above) and female heads (below), which is a privileged vantage-point over the exceptional urban space which surrounds the building. The façade ends in a balustrade, which serves as a counterpoint to the unbroken first-floor balcony, while the ground floor and entresol form an independent unit, barely connected to the upper floors by some decorative elements (a head of Mercury, a griffin and a winged lion), which link the top of the entresol windows with the balcony on the first floor. The central axis is subtly marked on the façade by the most highly wrought decorative element of all: the emblematic head of Mercury placed over the main entrance, the first-floor fronton, with an enigmatic crowned head, and the protruding second-floor balcony. The lantern on the roof is a further key to the central axis.

CASA PEDREÑO